This Thin Mean

New Selected Poems

Eric Hoffman

SPUYTEN DUYVIL
NEW YORK CITY

Certain of these poems were previously published in the Dos Madres Press collections *Life At Braintree* (2008), *The American Eye* (2011), and *Forms of Life* (2015). The Trakl translations originally appeared in the journal *otoliths*.

© 2019 Eric Hoffman
ISBN 978-1-949966-25-1

Library of Congress Cataloging-in-Publication Data

Names: Hoffman, Eric R., author
Title: This thin mean : new selected poems / Eric Hoffman.
Description: New York City : Spuyten Duyvil, [2019]
Identifiers: LCCN 2019006387 | ISBN 9781949966251
Classification: LCC PS3608.O47767 A6 2019 | DDC 811/.6--dc23
LC record available at https://lccn.loc.gov/2019006387

In memory of Paul Pines, 1941-2018

Forms of Life   1

(2014-2015)

The Vast Practical Engine   47

(2009-2010)

Life at Braintree   63

(2007-2008)

New Poems   89

(2017-2019)

Translations   123

(2018-2019)

Forms of Life

If the many become the same as the few when possess'd,
More! More! is the cry of the mistaken soul; less than
All cannot satisfy man.
        William Blake

1

The new lights dazzle and astonish—
Revolution's blazing comets
give flesh to ravaged spirits,
illuminate the fate of mankind—

It is a question of narrative:
nature has scattered life
in such profusion, yet is miserly
in cultivation

2

There is no exceeding our ability to feed—
Deny this and be burdened

with catastrophe,
with misery among all
no matter the inequality—

These dark tints are drawn from conviction,
not jaundiced eyes,
nor spleen of disposition

3

Necessity restrains,
plants and animals shrink
by waste of seed,
sickness, and insatiate death—

Numerous waste lands,
pastures and a butcher's meat—
Horses outdistance their sun—
Titan strength in the land,

instruments of our diminution,
a caprice of fashion,
and in this truth
one finds a kernel virtue

4

There is no limit to Earth
beyond its solar allotments,
the salt texture of its winds—

Its core of razor heat
radiates into ozone,
infuses plants and animals
impelled by instinct to increase
without doubt or interruption—

This urge is bolted into every edifice
repressed by nourishment,
the fear of the Neanderthal
or the small marsupial—

Hunter and hunted
etched in cavern walls by firelight

5

Amidst buildings and streets,
orderly progressions
of documents and laws,
of stagnant wages and higher rents,
impel a man to labor harder,

to eke out fortune or failure,
to be clothed in fineries or in rags,
to clamor for bread or for dividends,
to choose his charities
or to make himself a charity

6

Even in this vicious place,
virtuous attachments
grow strong, stronger even
than places of peace—

Hunters and gatherers,
the population dispersed, spread thin—
Nomad's passion less ardent,
diffuse as the men between them—

Settling in some fruitful spot,
the tribe relaxes into alien civility,
acquires children as fast as poverty,
their women chattel, resigned to slavery

7

Orphaned children crowd the street—
Merciless, accustomed
to barter and theft
so that they might survive—

Not simply the ruddiest,
even the pale and infirm,
the weak little starling
whose small heart flutters

8

Want is the goad
that drove Scythian shepherds
from their flock,
famishing wolves in search of prey—

A cloud of Barbarians
descend from the North,
their congregated bodies
blotting out the sun—

Young scions parceled out from parent-stock
given instruction to explore fresh regions,
to gain happier seats
by the gleam of their flashing swords

9

Want pinches the poor, desolation extends
its empty arms around them—

Their slow progress of numbers
cannot be traced

to the decay of passion,
undiminished in vigor

10

Rank on the ladder,
steps ascend or descend and,
depending on the degree of deprivation,

the stature one wants to attain,
the considerations are trivial
or contemplative—

A man will submit to harder fare
and labor for the sake of living
with a woman he loves,

for they will gladly give food
and the love of Christ
for one more thorn-bound soul

11

Corpses of Orcus—
Moldy patents—

The increase of one decreases the other,
and so they remain impoverished—

A seedling tyranny—
Evil gone too far to be remedied—

The poor fulfill their part
of an impossible obligation
we never intend to return—

They sacrifice liberty for nothing

12

We are in a savage state
despite our fair-sounding words,
the noble plumage of genius—

All we have are exertions
and some sleep—
Laughter that wounds all memory, a little death

13

The pride and self-deceptive expectations
of our children,
the diminishments of our kingdoms,
as when a vast fortune
falls victim to some complex
unexpected action,
its coffers emptied,
its fruit consumed by lechers,
all the blandishments of our best intentions
devoured by wolves

14

Skull drudgery, habits of mind
preclude the common vision—

We occupy an echo-worn
and darkened sphere,

an angry, shrill,
paranoiac and hysteric cry

that drowns out the still,
still voice of reason

15

There is error in supposing
the difficulty arising
is at a great distance—
The whole earth a cultivated garden—

Unlimited progress
from partial improvements—
A fallacy of limits—
An 'organic perfectibility of man'—

Who supposes?
If his natural facilities remain the same,
what will be the certainty—
The degree of hope

16

Things improve—
Refinements, adjustments,
the preponderance of evidence exposed
to the maw of human knowledge
that has no preference

for cordiality or sin—
Duration will increase without ceasing,
will have no assignable term—
All is indefinite,
A constant approach to unlimited extent—

The earth split by rivers—
The immensity is geologic—
Astounded by the expanse of the cave's mouth,
the slow cylinder of time
cauterized by its vaulted depths

17

That we may shut our eyes
to the Book of Nature,

return to old philosophies,
make facts bend to systems—

Tautologies—
Mystic pasts scratched on cavern walls

18

The wheelcart of the sun
and the sweat of the oxen,
the hundred tonne
gallon per second swing
of the river's arm
cools silent stones,
spins in eternal motion
the immense carved wheels
of the water house

19

Our ardor in pursuit—

The heavy mechanisms
that chain our mouths
to sugared tubers and fruits—

A beautiful system
of event and distance

20

The want for the child to grow,
for the wife to live,
of happiness weighed against misery,
of the sorrow of witness,
and the heart that wears its convictions—

Then comes the advent of happiness—
A necessary oscillation—
For men and women without children
are the loss of hope and
the erasure of all that it means to be human

21

Equality by reason
and not by force
is beautiful—
An amelioration among men—

The whole is little better
than a dream,
a beautiful phantom
of the imagination—

22

The turbid spring of human life—
No equality in plenty—
And if all had all,
all would suffer to guard his life,
a little storehouse,
until the earth refused absolutely
to produce more,
returning us to the dark days of nothing—

This presses upon us,
so that even utmost purity
collapses under hunger's weight
and its petty degradations

23

Crowds flee the pestilent cities—
Prolific husbandry in the hillsides
and the wealth of healthy gardens—

This beautiful fabric vanishes
at the severest touch of truth

24

The spirit of benevolence,
invigorated by plenty, repressed
by the chilling breath of want—

The hateful vanished passions,
the black train of vice—
Save for some mysterious interference of heaven—

Benevolence, not self-love—
A stripping away of impediments—
The heart's dark boundaries

25

Passion in an age is not consistent
with reason or virtue—

Ardor is arduous—

Who has felt at first
that insatiable hunger
without reason or cause,
or lust, if true,
has found a selfless lust
that appeals to more
than bestial urges—

The eye's refinement
is the most invigorating oxygen,
sanctuary from the inevitable—
Spontaneity's remnant

26

Miles of ice and snow,
purpose, indefatigable—

The mind's profession
as purveyor—
Then it can wander—

as when a horse of spirit,
half-tired, is stimulated by the spur
and the bit put upon his mettle

27

A jaguar flows between leaf and shadow
as blood through a vessel—

Its eyes wear savagery's fabric,
its breath the wet smoke of hunger—

When the jaguar steps,
The jungle holds its breath

28

Myriad centuries—
Myriad—
And the time that ripples through
the crowded stones of events—

The winnowed elements
that acquiesce to form
germinate
in the dimensions

29

Worlds and the tilted axes
on which they spin
revolve in equilibrium,
set on their perpetual ellipses—

Calculate the velocity of a falling body
in vacuo's persistence

30

Cause flows in the acme of perfection—
The florist prepares the flower
yet other suns
may produce a perfect pink
carnation and
a bursting flame may be a trifle

31

The young painter in his studio
makes his study from a sketch—

Should we say he benefits?
Unwisely he strains to imitate

the inimitable, and destroys
the intellect he means to improve

32

We have only the perfectibility
of imaginary numbers
that cannot hope to penetrate the core,
which is impenetrable if it exists,
and is always there—

The miracle of potential
each pebble portrays,
even in the frozen reaches
of the expanse, we find it
unalloyed

33

The chart of the miserable confrontation
between the heart and constant power—

Benevolence, the rays from his hand
A correction to nature's indifference

34

Engaged in ornamented luxuries,
a peculiar sense of civilization—
It is a numbers game,

imaginary and useless,
augmenting values
and not the mass of happiness—

Wealth supports, wealth rewards
without merit or decree,
and the arrogant endure

35

Artificers over husbandry,
the uncultivated lands
expand beyond
the Northern reaches—

So Price was correct:
The great cities
are the graves of mankind

36

A healthy young man
wedded to a voluptuous beauty
eager for children—

Such bounty
a bloom of youth
no effort can arrest

37

That which is most remote
but known to all,
a snow-capped peak,
an ethereal spark
encountering a clod of clay,
impressed upon
by a forming hand,
as cooperation charms
the cells into their intricate state,
as eyes strive for light,
and mouths surround
the empty core of hunger—

The mind's infancy
is a coordination of forms,
organs sewn into action,
the sinews of revelation

38

The savage would slumber
forever under his tree
unless roused from his torpor
by the cravings of hunger
or the pinching of cold—

The wants of the body
have given cause
to the noblest of exertions—

All are compelled
by blind necessity
and the pursuit of good
is without vicious propensity

39

These pieces of clay
receive distinct impressions,

an ardent love or disapprobation,
bright orbs and beaming lights,

life to unnumbered worlds,
lost and confounded

40

Clouds and tempests
darken the world—

All intellect
rises from a speck—

Miracles occur—
The touch of a torpedo—
And this vicious place is forever prepared
to dispose of wisdom

The Vast Practical Engine

1.

the wood must be
frost-bitten and
dry, the
seeds must wither
and decay,
the action of leaves
reverse

the fragmented world
is in ruin, the same
world
intact is born

 "never use the words
higher and lower" for

"the wind bloweth
where it listeth"

what is most continuous
is most profane, bundles
of observations

words and not world

the cosmos
is empty of idols

the universe
is weather

2.

o haunted and prolific world
of violent machinations—
you are no child,

you are a rock in the sun,
jaguar sheathed
in jungle leaves,

soft globule,
tender bead of sweat,
indifferent to an indifferent sun

3.

Swedenborg's Damascus
was a tavern
where he received celestial wisdom
from angels and apparitions

"I enjoy perfect inspiration"

yet for all his knowledge
of the geo-thermal core
he never found a hell
quite so punishing
as the human heart

said Emerson: "He turned the universe
into a gigantic crystal"
like some cosmological alchemist
"the universe in his poem
suffers under a magnetic sleep"—
reflects the magnetizer's mind

4.

All men are equal in their political rights
Negroes are men:
Negroes are equal in their political rights
            C.S. Peirce

Agassiz the empirical
the vast practical engine
in love with Morton's *crania*

the Caucasian burden
scribed in hollow bowl

far below, the Indian
"restless, vengeful, fond
of war, wholly destitute of
maritime adventure"

and the "joyous Negro,
resplendently simple in
his African sun,
his climate incompatible
with the intellect,
deleterious, his fat lips
and grimacing teeth,
the wool on his head,
his bent knees and
the livid color of his palms—"

Time
does not alter organized beings

God improved his hand
By fashioning a lighter kind,
yet Nachash, that black gardener,
waits with coiled urgency,
listens for a voice of childlike wonder
and joyous simplicity

5.

one cannot stop
to chase doubts
like rabbits
or to paint the surface
of law,
though it is cracked and rotten

God or reason,
edifices atop
mountains of data

the possibilities open,
Agassiz,
where you would
have them closing

6.

every bit of us
at every moment
is part of a wider self

quivering along
various radii

a compass wind rose

and the actual
is continuously one
with unseen possibles

7.

what are the physics
of violence? or

are we the embodiment
of need, our tenderness

merely an apparition
approximate

to appetite's defeat?

"There is no certainty
only those who are certain"

that the heart is small

that the world
cradles and destroys

that the triumph of breathing
rescues
and buries

8.

o my soul
Nothing but a child's cry

such purity in not knowing
but seeking knowledge

and once in its possession
it is only by degrees
knowing its mutability
and limits—

the lungs expel
and draw back in again

dangles above the dragon's mouth
licking honey

all vales dressed in mourning
all teeth in the museum
some fated living victim

forms of horror fill the world

even here in our hearths and gardens
an infernal cat plays with a panting mouse
or holds a hot bird
that flutters in her jaws

9.

the world is certain
yet we cannot know
for certain its certainty
is all there is
to be known

things *happen*
and Truth is a thing

10.

nothing is so precise
as imagination
but what demon

hides in the most
precise equations—
what infinitesimally

small loss occurs
at that invisible edge
maps the distance

between the mind of God
and the limits of
absolute reason

11.

the masonry's stone traces
ancestry, the efforts of
intention versus the weight

of rock against the mind that,
boneless, imagines no limits
to exertion, pressed between

the motory of flexion
and the force of a stubborn
permanence. Yet we are a

product of this radiance,
a pebble in the boulder's core,
the thin mean of survival,

a dynamic of the distance
from this monstrous indifference
to the smallest seed of hope

12.

mind engenders truth
upon reality

like the caramel glaze
upon a candy apple

it makes little difference
whether or not we say

a stone on the bottom of the ocean
is brilliant

that the stone may be fished up
tomorrow

yet there are gems
at the bottom of the sea

and flowers in the untrammeled desert

Life At Braintree

1.

When a fool has a prize
In his hands, he has no
Heart to improve it—

Little boats, water mills,
Wind mills, whirly Giggs,
Bird Eggs, Bows and Arrows,

Guns, singing, Pricking Tune,
Girls &c. Ignorance of Parents.
By a constant Dissipation

Among Amuzements, my Mind
Has laid uncultivated. Horace
And Homer—Proh Dolor!

2.

Life at Braintree: no newspapers,
No mails, no travellers, few books,
(And those to him wholly unreadable),

Sunday the sole holiday,
Church, tavern, and village store
The only resorts or amusements.

In the best houses the cold
Of the sitting rooms tempered
By huge, wooden fires, which roasts

One half of your body, while
The other half is exposed
To chilling drafts. Women

Wear shawls, men overcoats.
Bread freezes at the Lord's Table
And at night so too does the ink in its well.

3.

The Fields of Nature . . . the Flowers,
The Prospect of Forests and Meadows.
Songs and Girls . . . flutes, fiddles,
Concerts and Card Tables, original sin,
Origin of evil, the Plan of the Universe,
Want of the Breezes from the Sea
And the pure Zephyrs from the
Rocky Mountains of my native Town.

I cannot tolerate those who cannot
Distinguish between the aspirations
Of the sage and that of aspiring
Toward wisdom itself. I talk
About the folly of Love, about
Despising it, about being above it,
Pretending to be insensible of tender Passions,
And she only laughed. She practiced
The art of pleasing only—
Her heart and her face have no correspondence.

4.

Make observations: his Head bent forward,
His shoulders round and his Body
Writhed, his mouth large and irregular,
His teeth black and foul, and craggy,
His Visage long and lank, his
Complexion wan, his Cheeks fallen—
He is a Genius at popularity.

5.

A decision of the passions.
Contemptu Famae, Contemni Virtutem.
Iago makes the Reflection that Fame

Is but a breath, but vibrated Air,
An empty sound. Yet *Contemptu*
Famae, Contemni Virtutem.

Contemptu famae fama aguebatur.
This tyrants and villains always knew—
Their character weighs heavy on the world.

6.

A Life of Effeminacy, Indolence,
And Obscurity or a Life of Industry,
Temperance and Honour? Rise and mount

Your Horse by the Morning's dawn,
And shake away amidst the great
And beautiful scenes of Nature—

All the Crudities that are left
In your stomach, and all the obstructions
That are left in your Brains.

7.

Flowers for the most part:
People might be more practically
Or more sensuously stupid.

8.

Girl, gun, cards, flutes, violin, dress,
Tobacco, laziness, langour, inattention,
Pipe, poem, love letter . . . Law
And not Poetry is to be the Business
Of my life. Save for my Diana
To whom I am Lysander, she
Has so softened my heart.

9.

The people: ignorant of arts and letters,
Seldom able to frame and support
Regular opposition, gullible and slow

To resist tyranny. This settlement
Nevertheless represents the Opening
Of a grand scene and Design

In Providence, for the Illumination
Of the Ignorant and the Emancipation
Of the slavish Part of Mankind.

10.

We shall not execute witches
Or Quakers, nor shall we Brits.

A fair trial, besides, lends
Respectability for the cause.

11.

Farewell Politicks. Divide my time
Between Law and Husbandry.
Still calm, happy, Braintree.

The mistranslation of the Puritan
Concern over Salvation
Into the worthiness for success.

Yet in politicks the public
Judges worthiness. It procures
Me anxiety, and Obloquy enough.

12.

The air of Boston is not favourable
To me who passes my life
In the Country. A Pain in my Breast

And a complaint in my Lung.
I'd return to the Air of my native Spot
To mind my own Farm, and my own Office.

13.

Without the mind at ease, no health.
I have not wrote one Line
In a newspaper these two Years.
I grow weary of this idle,
Romantic jaunt. I want to hear
The news. I feel guilty, as if
I ought to be employed, for the Benefit
Of my fellow men. Edward and Alfred
Closed their long Glories with a Sigh to find
Th'unwilling Gratitude of base Mankind.
This has been the most flat, insipid,
Spiritless, tasteless Journey that I ever took.
I slumber, and moap away the Day.
Regardless of every Thing, yet to get Money
Enough to carry you smoothly through
This world. Year 1765, even at Midnight,
Over the Bowl or the Bottle? No,
Rebellion is a public confession
Of the wish for power. Hawthorne's
Molineux, 1773, an Epoch in History—
The closing of the port.

14.

I had a pretty Estate. A Lighter,
A Pew, an House in Boston.
Am I planning the Illustration
Of my family or the Welfare of my Country?

Each man's House is his Castle,
A compleat security, safety and Peace
And tranquility as it was surrounded
With Walls of Brass, with Ramparts
And Palisades and defended with
A Garrison and Artillery.

I did but prompt the age to quit their clogs
By the known Rules of ancient liberty,
When straight a barbarous noise environs me
Of owls and cuckoos, asses, apes, and dogs.

Passion and personal altercation.
Ambition without bounds.
Acrimony settled into Rancor and Malignity.

15.

Novanglus: Parliament has no power
Except by compact and consent.
A dissertation of conspiracy. A fallen
State of man. To abstain from English tea.

16.

Were we ever so happy? I dismiss
My Gard and grow weak, silly, vain,
Conceited, ostentatious. But a Check,
A frown, a sneer, a Sarcasm . . .
Makes me more careful and considerate.

17.

War and Desolation. Out of such Desolations,
Glory and Power, and Wonders may arise,
To carry on the Designs of Providence.

18.

Inquiry of the Founders of Empires
Consistent with European delicacy:
Our independence already exists!

19.

My nerves are tremulous tonight.
Wet with sweat. Pessimistic of
The democratic polis. Yet faith
In the efficacy of the people.

20.

Of that Ambition which has Power
For its Object, I don't believe
I have a Spark in my Heart.

21.

The honest Man is Seldom forsaken.
Pursuit by British frigates, two outsailed,

Third lost in the night: a hurricane
Split the mainmast; capture of prize ships,

Coming under fire. Braced against bed boards,
To prevent us from being dashed

Against the Plants and Timbers.
On deck, the smoke from enemy ship,

A plume of white dust, sulfur in the nose.
May the Design of my Voyage be answered.

22.

The treaty already answered. Hence, Bordeaux.
All my Voyages and Negotiations a Commedy.

The study of a society designed to answer
All the senses at once. Chat at coffee shop,

Play by Molière. At table, bosoms exposed.
Such attention to luxury. The Lights of a Calf

Dressed one Way and Liver another, and
The most delicate Raisins I ever saw. And

Madame de Texel, there was a Physical quality
In Us resembling the Power of Electricity

Or the Magnet, by which when a Pair
Approached within a striking distance

They flew together like the Needle to the Pole
Or like two Objects in electric Experiments.

23.

I cannot help loving these people. And that great
And good man, years before, falling asleep
While discussing the healthful properties of fresh air.
In his coonskin cap, playing the part of a simpleton.
Modesty is a virtue that can never thrive
In public. A man must be a Trumpeter
To perpetuate his Fame.

                                          Boarding at Nantes,
In dull cabin for weeks. Then home.
There is no Art nor Design to my life.

New Poems

Paul was converted
by light from Heaven,

Kyogen by stone
striking bamboo

His word was in mine heart
as a burning fire shut up in my bones.
Thus saith the Holy Ghost:
my hand slew them,
my finger stabbed them,
my nails cut them to pieces.

God's agent is slow to anger.
The wounds are corporeal,
inflicted by a broad hand
that sweeps categorically,
limitless, indiscriminate—
claiming innocence and sin alike.

Wisdom weeps
while wriggling worms
writhe under Yggdrasil,
old misshapen horses

wander past Irish bogs.
The ash tree decays, its agonies
branch, flower into heaven,
bury noxious roots in hell.

This is the place of the dragon
slain on the Knowth Stone,
and of the Connemara Peiste,
a weight on the souls of Men.

The universe is unlivable—
This crystal speech we occupy
too is unlivable—

The dead do not know
they are dead,
seed returned to seed—

To feel life burst forth,
the muscular snake thrust
in the quiet chamber,

yolk tremble in the tender shell.
Barbarous, external,
matter, now moral, within.

The incoming missile is quaint,
accomplishes what it intends:
a pinpointed, concussive punch.

It is abrupt, how an esplanade
is made a cemetery
in the time it takes.

War is bland epiphany,
wrecks door frames
in which they cower and linger,

and plead, relieved in a way
to be absolved of waiting for mercy.
And to manage their escape.

Men who make art in old age
are foolish perhaps—
There are no longer any beautiful
young women to listen
in rapture to his impassioned pleas,
or to make his inadequacies
seem noble and brave.

The hardened hands
of the old farmer
do not soften,
though he grasps after
with the village maiden.

No ghosts appear to us,
no duty of vengeance
is laid at our feet,

no lover drowns from grief,
no dead father goes unavenged.
No knife, no stage, no words.

Here on the western inlet,
the trees and water are dark.

Wind blows through the pines,
water caresses the shore.

Animals move in the shadows,
elusive, legendary.

Still water reflects the house lights,
a final, temporary glimpse

of an end to immensity,
a faceless voice, a meridian silence.

The eyes of the deer
clenched, muscled heart—

Gone like a shot
echoes in a quiet clearing—

They ring like smoke
in the snowstorm dark—

A bullet from its cavity—
Your heart the heat

from an unassailable wound
defends my resurrection—

Echoes from the valley
dance from hill to hill

and cleave the wind—
Trembles, newly risen—

Arrange leaves and sticks,
prop them against the sun

and sift for words
to describe.

This bright flame cradles,
glistens in limbs,

an opake ball
of molten gold

teases black & green.
A waiting frames all.

Listen.
Quietly we step

over summer grass,
shoes in hand. Blades

caress our naked feet.
The onset of night carefully

falls. The measured syllables,
perfect as joists

set in weakened dirt
with wooden strength

that temporal hurt
cannot restrain.

wingéd ants
in the damp road
after rain,

fleets of bees
in the silvering
circular space

a white hardhack
out of bloom
by the stone pile—

sweet briar
from the woods
growing in the yard—

an elevated sea-beech
within reach
of marine influences

rays of morning sun
light shrub willows
by the muddy river

the turtle's tough infancy
makes ridiculous our life
of disease and low spirits

cast steel soap galls
straddled on twigs
dropping from shrub oaks—

is not Art a gall?
the seed of man
planted in nature

and stung by God—
anticipated
at oak's creation,

so the canoe
when birch was made.
genius strings nature

wayward the tendril
pauses obligates
to the substantial
vegetable growth

am I this strength
seeded in the muscle?
the center of the rock
cores energies—

    it knows
this obliteration
as bones know stone
hardness to their shape

what is owed
to one's self?
a measure dances
on a precipice

      unfolds
resolute as stone
silent as the core
obligation seeds

Above an empty field—
winter sun, silent snow

Amos 5: 8-24

in some seson whenne softe was the sunne

All mercies shrivel,
all boasts of nations erase,

the massive anthems become a broken choir
muted hymns cannot place.

1.

Scribes tend to mercantilism, the peasantry pursues starvation.
The unlettered aristocracy tend to militaristic fame,

to defend, they say, the civilian population
from foreign aristocrats in search of venal glory.

We cannot all be kings and queens
and run the nation like a slum, an inherited debt.

Vaults are made the graves of dead currencies;
all is beggarly outside the master's kitchen.

The most insignificant arrear serves as the small mean
between the barest subsistence and personal luxury.

They devour themselves and succor on freedom,
the ultimate price of vigilance.

Plunder and murder, quietly legalized,
keeps the grease from cobwebbed guillotines.

The slick-booted patrolman roars,
declares the absolute right of righteous annihilation.

2.

Amos, tasked with the difficult mission
of condemnation in a smooth season, was ignored.

Many said intelligent things they knew to be true
and saw strange things in the distance –

why must one peer into darkness for truth
when the lies are so brilliantly illuminated?

All data is observation, all politick disillusion and distortion.
A cry went up where there would be heaven.

Righteous indignation is the luxury of the rabble masses.
What sunders us must also piece us together.

3.

We intend to distinguish ourselves from the merely topographic,
from that shining deity who makes marginal the stars of heaven.

We cannot speak properly of paradise, for we are not there.
We color blind force with reckoning.

The Word is the thinnest possible surface,
the truest point of a blade.

Prophecy is poetry, particular and demanding.
The true prophet speaks harshly when hope is still alive.

The prophet's words are a burden instead of a flame.
When the prophets speak, they do not listen.

They eye the swift horses that loiter in the corral,
and in fleeing risk the death of little children.

4.

The gate bar of Damascus is broken.
The world is on fire with the heat of resignation.

Passion consumes it, the blind force of judgment,
the Earth drilled with Elizabethan ruff,

clouds of tornadoes in fists that clutch rags of confusion,
shining stupidities mistaken for God.

The torrents of primeval waters do not hear it.
Nor do the animals fixed in the hunt or dazed with sleep,

nor the frigid vast palaces of light in the remote alpine,
nor the ocean's alien deep, nor the frozen millennia.

5.

Turmoil persists in the company of ghosts.
Stones swell and flowers speak. The earth thirsts.

A massive upheaval of sea cascades,
high as the topmast a thousand waves.

We, the drifting chaff,
are swept away in the monstrous torrent of dismissive spit.

Yet comes a cry from the Fish Gate, and from the Second Quarter,
thunder from the hills as the Mortar people wail.

From afar, observers watch from the Serene Sea,
centered upon its apex,

an assemblage of the Chiaroscurans
above the pyramid's slopes.

6.

Determinate evil in ferric waters, alkaline, unveiled,
swirls of porous yolky eyes, opaque, and grim.

Birds of air and fish of sea rendered sacrificial.
Christened with ash, teeth gnash and wail.

The emplacements lie in ruins, the city streets in ruins,
the detritus cries of emptiness

while houses and shops teem with nothing.
The winds and seas have tossed us, our spear hands grow weary.

The once fertile fields are ribbed with barrenness,
the oceans choked with industry.

The seas burn to vapor, blossoms wither and fade.
The hills melt under the weight of heat,

the ground buckles and roils with quakes.
None can endure the wraith-like fire.

The ancient stones of the western hills
shatter like cannonballs thrust at metal hulls.

An oak submerged beneath the waters
remains an oak, its skin made opaque

by the murky depths, as though bones were crystal
and the dirt that covers them invisible—

their empty eyes gaze eternally into vacant skies.
The labyrinthine chasm yawns.

7.

The weakest seeks release
from the wreckage of good intent.

Children abandoned, their fingers, weak, cling tenaciously
to the minor triumph of inglorious spoiled rags.

Judgment reigns the broken dead.
The void of their eyes consumes everything.

Their emptiness amputates the living.
Their houses plundered, their wealth laid waste.

The last day hastens, breaks in the blood red dawn.
Complacency boils in the absence of an enemy's guilt.

The warrior throws down his sword and wails
ruination, unending ruination, darkness, and gloom.

Defeat, the rotted bodies of our brothers,
our only peace a seized thresher.

The city is desolation, its citizenry disconsolate.
Noon is uprooted from the clocks.

The poisoned world is a relic of polity, a rain of blasts,
an home of rubble, desolation.

Blinded, they feel the sting of wind on shorn faces.
Muted, they scream with their eyes.

Wounded, they remove steel
from the hot cavity of flesh.

8.

Our lives are a disorderly archive.
Our flesh falls away like the walls of a conquered city.

Pain is cradled in the nerves,
the same loathsome darkness that enfolds us.

What blue ruin will the fallen walls display
when at last the desperate shadows retreat?

Distress that nothing conveys the mind's contents,
neither the body nor its prayers they are obliged to hear,

obscured by the blast of trumpets
and the footfall of millions.

Blood will turn the dust to mud
and the flesh will stink like shit.

9.

Must they bring us to nothing in order to save us?
And we who cannot speak of paradise,

for we are not there, can it not speak or think of us?
A fraction of infinity is still infinity.

They laughed at lame Hephaistos
as he hobbled 'round the great table, pouring nectar.

What will they make of us, as we crowd
the bitten fields, soiled, defiled, oppressed?

We who took no correction,
who refused to trust and humble ourselves before them?

We are those who carry the crosses and flags,
and in battle assume the shape of the liberty bell.

We remain unified in hope of conveyance of the geometric,
companioned to a few simple words

as guide and comfort in this vast wilderness,
occluded and lost.

10.

We dig our way into hell.
and the life-giving waters consume the flesh,

the nourishing sun scorches the Earth.
The soils deplete. The harvest starves.

White dust collects on the heads of the wretched.
Their survival is the small hook

that pierces the fiercest shark
and brings him to submission

to the pain of the hook, worsened considerably
by the intensity of his thrashing.

11.

We are the skeleton's soft marionettes.
We have journeyed from wilderness to wilderness.

We will taste the corrosives that replace water.
We will hear the roar of the lion without prey.

We will see the ensnared peregrine struggle for release
and the children like mice removed from its unforgiving talons.

12.

Are we the only family the universe has known?
Can that fathomless expanse clotted with immensities,

with unchartable distances that outlast the measure of time,
diminish itself enough to perceive our insignificance?

Is the broad desert concerned with a mote of dust?
The ocean with one single-celled prokaryote?

Is the ineffable simply another drab task of a clerk?
Our words are chalk to the limestone.

We collect our zones, our longitudinal forces,
the wooden gyres and steel pendulums, and assign their motions.

None shall know the cause of the fractures,
from earthquake, or war, or the slow cylinder of time

that has invisibly picked the wall apart piece by piece
and hidden the remnants where none can find them.

13.

There is the clean teeth that have bread to eat,
the child with the breast to nuzzle.

There is sun to nourish them.
There is earth rich with minerals.

There is rain on the crops and on the crops of your neighbor.
There is the mountain, and there is the wine to drink,

there is the feast that requires no sacrifice.
Everyone drinks, from none is the taste withheld.

Nothing is withheld but dread.
The blight is an unreal memory.

The gardens increase, the vineyards, and fruit trees.
The captive horses carry their riders willingly.

The plagues remain in a distant country.
The weaponry's trajectory becomes confused.

14.

Morning is always dark upon the plains.
The wind, untethered from the world,

fashions the thunderhead, paints sound
throughout the valley, in the branches of the pines

and among the switches and hedgerows.
The abandoned city sits forlorn upon the horizon,

a silhouette of bankrupt concepts, a geometric pillar of ash,
its gleaming towers footnotes to the vaulted caverns

where old stones count the millennia
as though they were a single drop of rain.

15.

No one knows the things of God.
He breaks out like a fire among the ashes.

He demands repentance.
Master, and slave. Slave, and master.

He comes between us as reconciliation,
as though righteousness can be commanded,

or hunger tempered, or the child's screams
met with anything other than agony.

He turns the shadow of death into morning?
We lay waste to the death of morning

by the eye's insatiable hunger for the light.
He made the Pleiades and Orion, yet so did we.

The internal-combustion engine,
then animal pragmatism, then nothing.

Tipping points, by degrees, achieved
on a quark or gluon scale, unobserved.

A diamond that survived the ordeals,
a salamander that lives in the fire.

16.

The poet's ashes are scattered near the pyramid
of Caius Cestius, somewhere near Rome,

who spoke of the remnant statue
whose contours are a testament to civilization,

who made the poor the packhorses of taxes.
The granaries are empty, the glebes have withered.

All is dry dust and depletion, a monochrome of brown
stippled with osiers, a plain pockmarked with yawning thirst.

Bees wander in a hungry daze, the tint of delirium
in the small lenses of their five eyes,

compositions of blue and gray, synthesis and dissolution,
desultory lights, local congeries of protoplasmic eggs.

Nailed to the wall, left to molder and wither,
like Bacon's library at Oxford, an orderly forest,

bric-a-brac democracies shed.
The moralist must now be the devil.

Monks with skulls in their cells,
the beautiful bone in fixed jest,

a firebrand plucked from the fire,
a broken cromlech among the ruins.

Translations

From Isaiah

1.

Hear, heavens, give ear, Earth—
My children, nourished, rebel.
An ox knows its owner, an ass
Its master's crib, yet Israel
Is unknown to its people.
Iniquity, evil's seed, corrupts the young

Gone away backward.
What purpose is this revolt?
The head is sick, the heart faint,
The body wounded, bruised and untended.
Desolation reigns in the countryside,
And the cities burn with fire.

Strangers invade and devour.
Zion's daughter a vineyard cottage,
A lodge in a cucumber garden, a city besieged.
We are left with remnants
Unlike Sodom, unlike Gomorrah,
And a voice comes down like thunder:

What purpose is sacrifice?
What delight is blood?
Who brings you before me
To crowd my court, and beg judgment?
No more vain oblations, new moons,
Sabbaths and assemblies,

Even solemn meetings are iniquity.
Your hands are full of blood.
I hide my eyes from you.
Seek judgment. Relieve the fatherless.
Plead for the widow.
Your sins, red as scarlet, as crimson,

I will make as the fresh fallen snow, as wool.
The obedient shall eat,
And the rebellious shall meet my sword.
Avenge me and I will purge you of sin,
I will restore the first judges
And the city redeemed shall rise from ash.

The cities fill with judgment,
The once-righteous become murderers,
Silver is made dross, wine thinned by water.
Princes are companions with thieves,
They abandon the fatherless, the widowed.
So the voice thunders again:

And the crooked shall be ashamed of the oaks
They desired, and the gardens they chose.
They shall be faded as an oak leaf,
Parched as gardens without water.
The strong will light the spark
In which, desiccated, enflamed, they burn.

2.

We will be taught the ways,
We will walk the path,
Beat our swords into ploughshares,
No war between nation and nation.
The land is rich with gold and silver and horses.
There is no end to their chariots and treasures.

Who among them is unaccountable?
Everyone with breath in his nostril.
Yet they are made mean by trinkets and jewels.
They make and do unforgiveable things.
Judgment hunts them, trembling,
Unrepentant, they hide in the earth,

The proud and lofty brought low,
They will give their silver and gold
To the moles and bats, and
They will hide in the ragged rocks
And caves and hide in the dust.
He will shake the earth to find them.

Judgment will come to the cedars of Lebanon,
To the oaks of Bashan,
To the high mountains and the hills.
Judgment, to the high towers
And every fenced wall, and to the ships of Tarshish,
And upon all pleasant pictures.

After Ozaki

Pail dipped in water—willow shadow broken every time

Cicadas sing—one, two three—morning ferry

Lanterns lit, he heads home—mountain graves

Persimmons ripen in the sea's salt wind—fishing village

Tea shop shōji: 'kotatsu inside'

We've separated—in loneliness I break wild chrysanthemums

In a dead garden, mountain tea flowers bloom

Windows open, dawn illumines the sea

Evening—I write a letter in hotel light

The sea grows dark, yet red lights brighten

Among school-children, ocean waves crash at our feet

Dawn—forest bathed by a passing rain

A lady draws near, lamplight illumines her eyes

Blackened sea sleeps—arrival at a quiet inn

Morning—a girl opens her window

Scream heard in darkness, someone runs away

Wet footbridge—rain brightens the sky

Spring flower blossoms—morning air chills petal shadows

Warm night—reflection of stars in shallow pools

The child who loves to cry can cry again

Immense crematory smokestack burns the insignificant dead

Scentless yellow flowers belong to the Buddha

Bells at dusk, I walk by

Frost at nightfall—wooden beams creak

Wife away from home, shōji darkens

Warm sun melts snow, touches and brightens children's cries

In pain, I write a letter with one lonely eye

Red tufts hang precariously from the horse cart

Dusk at New Year's Day—evening lamp lit, quietly

Spring night—smoke fires lengthen

Bamboo forest—cold light of morning

Guided by tide, orange and yellow lanterns of the boats

Fish vendors—sunlight for sale

I smell the earth to determine what will sprout

She kneads my back; what occupies her thoughts?

Left on the table, festival chrysanthemum

Our intimate words, whispered immensities in the mountain depths

Child's hand, small in my palm, held carefully

Sunset—brush stroke swept across the sky

Poppies cut for the Buddha continue to bloom

Green pine in sunlight, rows of graves in sand

Morning after storm—chrysanthemums bloom

Stormy sky—in the distance a bell rings

Wind too strong to light a match—we speak in that cold

The sunflowers bow toward my evening desk

Tired of arguing, I walk outside into the hot sun

Temple roofs, mountain top—as I descend, autumn leaves fall

Funeral at twilight—all is blue

Outside, children crying, lanterns lit in the houses

Refuge from wind and rain—in clenched fists, warm coins

Withered field—footsteps accumulate

Hole carved in ice, fishing line disappears

Horse led down a frozen road, head hung low

At stream's edge, melted ice begins to flow

Small window, massive storm—apricots fall

The smoke from the afternoon fires keeps the woods at a distance

A favorite bridge has burned down—I will miss it

In April sun, the villagers assemble a house from clay

A horse, wild from pain, bolts across an icy field

Chimney smoke stirred by ceaseless wind

Mother's Day—people come and go

A new straw hat—water lilies stirred by warm noon wind

A dog passes by a broken fence, looks in—dull afternoon

A sick, dying man listens to the report of arms

A mother of many children crosses the great ocean

Mid-afternoon—a distant ship approaches, its deck is empty

Snow-white rice balls washed in mountain water

Returning home, immersed in darkness

Man sweeps fallen leaves—just beyond, a road to nowhere

Ships at sea, the snow-capped mountains remain

I move, my shadow moves—loneliness

Everyone at work— shōji left open

I pour tea for my guest—so, too, does my shadow

Ancient stone bridge—flowers fleeting

Evening sun—with what strength remains, I chase a horse

A leaf falls, someone laughs

At midnight I begin a long letter

Balanced on a blade of grass beneath an infinite sky, an ant

Rain tomorrow—I close the temple, ringed by green leaves

Today I am silent—butterfly's shadow

Rain all day—holy candles lit—I remain alone

I walk along the sandy shore—looking back, footprints vanished

In a quiet forest, a single leaf

In the well's darkness, my face reflects

Silent pond—a turtle surfaces

Bell rung—its hum accompanies my departure

The world's culmination—ants beneath a fiery sky

Sunset—mountain graveyard leans toward the sea

Narrow kitchen—not even room enough for my sleeves

Buddha's rice, pale white, only the mosquitos approach

Now I am as alone as the evening sky

Rainy day—nothing to be done but wander these sacred halls

Wakened from a nap—even the shadows are tired

Emaciated, whisking away bamboo leaves

Festival at dusk—the lanterns folded, collapse

I wear a chillba hat and pretend to forget everything

Afternoon bell oppresses—mimosa flowers

Buckets of spring water in both hands—I pass a dark road

Wordless, father and son go about their day—morning glories blossom

I step over a dead snake—sunset

The curtains are lowered—white fingertips

White sun in the sky, thick crematorium smoke

Backyard wooden gate—in, out—morning glories return to seed

Still forgotten, a black umbrella

White of the morning glory—endless

I place the bamboo basket on a bed of sun-drenched pine needles

Tadpoles multiply, summer garden

Children return from the hills with nuts—how do they find so many?

A beggar's child empties his bag of gingko nuts—there are hundreds

I follow the sound of water hidden in the fog

An old house, one room illuminated—someone's guest

Evening—a one-legged sparrow hops

Calm stream—I prolong my journey across the bridge

Dark sky—an ant journeys across my tatami mat

I kill an ant and in response more ants appear

Days of rain—the sparrows and I sit idly watching

Brand new chillba—shall we go out to sea?

Dawn—spilled rice beside the Buddha altar

I read yesterday's news, slap afternoon mosquitoes

I shell beans, decide to be kind

Holy lamp oil boils—impermanence

Harvested field—a crow's face up close

No blood, no complaints

Shōji closed, loneliness fulfilled

One stone placed in the garden—sunset

Autumn leaves scatter along the cold shore

Gravestone washed, he fans his face and neck

Straw roof—grass grows, flowers bloom

Waking dream forgotten, I weed the garden

I place zori on the child's foot, then release him to the autumn sky

Snap—thong broken in darkness

Wheelbarrow full of earth, my shadow silent

Ballons flutter in a breeze, their shadows flutter—they pass by quickly

Completely broke, and my nose is cold

Dusk—matchstick stuck deep in my ear

Old socks retain the shape of my feet

Many eyes study the sun-drenched monument

Chestnuts fall—the child and I listen

I burn leaves at evening, watch them flash their fiery tongues

I wander off, in my wake the sound of burning leaves

Dead leaves cling to my zori—I hang them out to dry

Daybreak—the waves arrive with regularity

Evening already, and only a brief glimpse of blue sky

A big sky just above me—my head is bare

A child watches as I fashion him a small wooden box

Sunlight—sawdust accumulates

Dead leaves burn, smoke stings the eyes

Chimney smoke in the living room—I open an old window

The stone Buddha sits motionless

One set of footsteps approaches—a small child

I remove my socks and toss the pebble

A child returns from the field—his face says 'I caught this'

In a tea shop—daylight hours only—the patrons sing

The horse bows—his massive legs fold

Bended nail, hammer off-center

A crow, in silence, departs

Mosquitoes—alone and cold, for how long will I be bothered?

With only this small brazier I struggle through the long winter

Morning—I sweep among the garden rocks

A few more days' reprieve from worship of the Buddha, I do the laundry

Radishes fatten—day and night I attend to the Buddha

The wind, my sole companion, blows all day long, causes me unrest

In darkness, I struggle to fit the key into the keyhole

The clarity of the stars is sobering

Preoccupied, I walk the length of the bridge without noticing

At supper, I sit on the wooden floor, my knees neatly folded

The moon so clear—I watch it alone, then fall asleep

Bamboo leaves flutter in the wind—I hope for a familiar companion

Loneliness—I spread open my five fingers just to look at them

Mismatched tongs—this will be a long winter

He rubs his bare foot against her bare foot—island woman

Head hung low, I walk despondently, and regret everything

Walking the halls filled with autumn wind, a solitary figure

Chrysanthemums strewn—midnight moon

A woman wearing dark glasses rests upon a stone—nothing more

Warm rag hung from a nail—frigid weather today

I close the temple hall—hundreds of sparrows return

Ant hole—nothing comes, nothing goes

Rainfall—garden stream—desolation

A murder tonight—and yet the water continues to flow

Water puddle ripples—slight evening wind

Stubborn needle cannot thread, I turn my gaze to the blue sky

I wear a winter hat— there's nothing left to say

In winter, this path goes nowhere

Onions grow large and the house deepens its evening roots

The sick man sleeps—I wind the clock that hangs from the pillar

Evening—I walk the same road with the same borrowed umbrella

Sweeping the small garden, I hear a baby's cries

Evening, the tall pine darkens—my bare feet need washing

I hold a sparrow in my hands feeling its warmth, then gently let it go

With no one to talk to, I retrieve a needle from the ashes

Gate closes, creaks noisily—the temple goes to sleep

I visit with my niece, let the umbrella resound with rain

I wear everything I own, yet still come down with a cold

Persimmons fall—we discuss what is

Chilly evening, black sash tied tight

December evening and only one cold bed

Kindling assumes the shape of my furniture

Snowfall on embers—morning

Hands frozen, he counts my winter perch

The persimmon seller counts her profits

Chewing on an unripened pear—argument

I grow old, imprisoned by deafness

Large family—each of the children reads from a different book

I mow the lawn, backyard gate left open

The ink blotter no longer absorbs my writings

'Salt the pickles in the jar!'—for this I was born?

Egg laid, retrieved—feel its warmth in my palm

Empty eggshell—I blow on it and it rolls away

Climbed down into a deep ravine—sunlight brightens

I cannot tell if she is laughing or crying

Pond drained, a puddle is all that remains—cold moon

Open the noisy gate and go out among the silent, brilliant stars

Dusk—a horse vanishes

Pond ice—only the children can guess its thickness

She has come all this way just to whisper a secret in his ear

The day darkens—I hurry to remove my funeral clothes

I watch the hail accumulate at the water's edge,
                                       then enter the hot spring village

Midnight—in the distance the sliding doors close

Light snow on street lamps—a woman has abandoned me

Winter tea shop guest, nothing left to eat

The waves lap against her heavy breasts

I walk the dog along the moat and the sky fills with snow

Snow falls into the dark river and in silence disappears

He knocks loudly at the snow-covered door, then enters

His dead body lies beneath a heavy stone stele

Snowflakes fall, scattered by flame

Winter light on an unopened door

Mountain path found, the water wheel turns

Lighthouses line the winter shore where I catch small fish—
                                       everything else is dead

I walk quickly along a snow-covered road

Muddy shoes removed, I take my place far from the Buddha

Mountain snow melts, I gather some fallen branches

Garbage thrown into winter river—I return home

The door firmly bolted—chilly night

A woman churns a handmill, sings to herself softly

The look of recognition still apparent on her face, she lights the charcoal

Daybreak, powerful waves, a clear blue sky—all are here before me

They sit together closely and speak in whispers—a wisteria dwindles

A cloudy day begins and ends in darkness—the sparrows also darken

Ground hardened by frost, even the worms have stopped crawling

I walk a frozen road, my clog straps loosened

Frosty morning, I scold a dog

My beard lengthens, I don my brazier

Steep waves, a towline tightens

Dead potted tree removed leaves a deep hollow

Night before the festival—lanterns lit, streets empty

On my return, the handkerchief still lies where it fell

Old enemy's face—I kick a stray pebble

I try to spoon water with a rusted out dipper

Nervous temple swallow, its dish is empty

I open the empty desk drawer knowing it is empty

Two chickens—all that remains in the morning snow

Late January, stone jizō beneath the tree—deep snow

Morning—I pick my teeth with a pine needle

Master's house—familiar gate

Evening—a sky of snow becomes a crow and darkens

Pure white shōji and the call of winter cranes—I am sound asleep

From a hot bath a face blossoms

Small guest room—the vast sea seen from a window

Cosmos above small hut

Supper's done, yet some daylight remains—a gift

An empty room looks out upon the sea

Unexpectedly I find a photograph from my childhood

The weather today is of a single face

Train to Tomatsu—raindrops cling to the window

Like a child, I hang from a bare oak tree

I became a body of the night—shisatsu bell

Morning—I enter the snow-covered town

A lonely woman—new year in the hot spring village

Deep autumn—small bird floats in pond

The bowl is hard and white

I work under a winter sky and wear a fragrant scent

Glaring sun—white face in window

I miss the fire that has gone to live in the sky

I hide in the blue of colored pencils

All the moon's ships have run ashore

Hotarukari Pond, small evening wave

A train passes as I weed the grass—I don't look up

Head shaved, I return home—the plums have fallen

Time passes, the temple falls into decay

We try to say goodbye yet the wind prevents it

Face red and wet, the child stops crying

The mountain greens and the path reappears

Small town newspaper takes only moments to read

I recognize the eyes of the alley cat

Alone in the temple shaken by an earthquake

Midnight—alone at a hot spring, I splash water on my belly

I stare at garden weeds as though bedridden

Beans swell in spring water—evening

In silence, a thousand ants appear

Headed home—umbrella on my shoulder as I cross the bridge

Laughter—teeth increase!

He opens the door to the temple kitchen—face like a peasant's

Every nail in the box is crooked

Beans to cook—I have more daylight than water

Village fabric store—ocean of calm

I awake to see the spider's slow descent

It is easy to weed rainsoaked ground

Solemn morning—three or four bamboo threads

Frogs croak—I turn off the lamp and go to sleep

Pond illuminated by the morning sun

Mind emptied—eyes wide open

Rough sea approaches a small bridge

Nails grow from my lonely body

Grassy countryside, we greet one another

The day ends, I lie on my stomach

The sea is blue, I'm at the barber's

I pass by a pond—my reflection is a stranger

I visit the monk, something's cooking in a pot

Mountain pass—light on Yamadera

I smell the rose and show it to you

Under the eaves, a spider catches a dragonfly

You, heating the bathwater, you're the one I want to see

New Year's Eve—now the calendar is old

Island sunset—fish leap from the sea

I write an impromptu note before returning home

I walk the beach—how long has that dog been following me?

I drink sake with the mountain priest—round moon

Moonlit night—I comb my hair

Perfect breasts and a mosquito

A storm approaches a bridge at dawn—lone willow

Stormy night—mother and child cling together

After the storm, a fool comes to sell us fish

My feet grow white as I wash them

Firefly dims, stops moving

I gave the largest pine tree to the sparrows, what remains is mine

A small window with a slight view of the sea

Pleased by my reflection, I purchase the mirror

The sea is so far away that we cannot hear the waves or tell if it is blue

I cannot stop thinking of the chickens' red wings

My skinny body only seems to make the mosquitos hungrier

A dragonfly drops by to visit me at my desk

Late night—barley powder spilled on the tatami mat

To cook the beans—pine cone kindling

It's wet by the well—evening wind

All the lonely villages visible from the mountain top

I stopped by only to get rid of the raindrops

You cry and I threaten you with tears

Hundreds of flowers bloom, all of them for sale

Autumn wind—stones tell of a child's birth

I look for discarded watermelons to eat—I'm going to grow fat

The woman in the newspaper clipping on the wall is always crying

For some, a sea breeze always pierces

Only the sound of wind while I draw water

While I slept, the rats ate all the potatoes

Night spent under bonsai, I return to Kokyō

I buy a goldfish for a small sick child

Wind blows around the house—no flowers

There is a view from the back window only

Sun sets on the naked sea and mountain

Water drank, I go outside to piss in the weeds

Where fireworks explode, that's where the town is

Early morning darkness—I search for a single flea

Althea flowers crumble in the wind

I could not outrun the wind

Shōji, filled with holes, shut tight

Strange location for a road, hidden in the tall autumn grass

I guide an eyeless man, who clutches at my shoulders

Morning—a flower blooms forth from lotus leaves

A sick patient watches as I cut the flowers

A beggar uses the flag as a sling

I buy two eggs, one for each pocket, then head home

Shrine festival—the baby remains asleep

Before sunrise, a wet crow flies

Mendicant with a walking stick passes by, praises my flowers

Headed home from the funeral, caught in the rain

A smoky pipe points the way

Recovered enough to arrange the cut flowers

I am as lost as a stray dog

Planted radish seeds, then vanished

Autumn already—the mountain leans toward my desk

The prostitute watches a child catch frogs

Over time, the sound of the rainfall changes

Shōji left open—the sea also darkens

Morning dew—I lead the bulls up the mountainside

Sparrow on a tatami mat—I recognize its footsteps

While sweeping I discuss the weather with the morning sparrow

A sky made blue by storm

Morning wind, flowers on the windowsill

Alone, but at least the fever's gone

From my bed I see the fire in the brazier increase

Devotions spoken into the blowing wind

In a small house, I speak with a mother and child

I go to bed without a book—loneliness

Dusk—the setting sun bathes the bamboo shoots

Moon, wind, night, loneliness—I cough

Pot of boiled rice—noise from the rim

Alone in a house—one or two fireflies drop by

I walk a mountain path, a small bird flies by

The sparrows have been busy here

Flowers in bloom, the child stays at home

Nails cut—I have ten fingers

Ship after ship arrive—one island

Fruit of the rose-flower—also lonely

Nightfall—waiting I place my hand on the skin of a tree

Child carried on my back—I place him on the sun-warmed stone

Small flower on a floating weed blossoms like a child

I look through the hole in the shōji—no one's home

Gorgeous morning—a pilgrim rings her bell

Without a bowl, I receive in both hands

Moon at dawn—storm comes ashore

Dead shijimi—mouth closed

Coughing—still alone

Wildfire—a train races by

Pliers placed on the tatami, quietly

Through faded chrysanthemums a part of the sea appears

I walk along the stream and stop

Out at sea in the wind and snow

Almost caught a dragonfly by its tail

Home from the cemetery, always alone

Forty years old, and I still love the pampas grass

Look out the window—what a round moon

This morning I use the water dipper and find its bottom rotted out

The wind dies down—pine needles fall

Winter—just passed the stone bridge

Autumn leaves in an azure sky

Wheat sewn, the wind never dies down

A field of rain next door too

Cold shaved head, frozen empty sky

Work begins at night—the sound of the river

The beggar arrived at just the right moment

Out on the cold sea, we lower the sails

I open the shōji to buy some fish

The pine cone as it is has become fire

The green grass, wind-blown

The evening storm dies down—I drink hot water

Deep snow—sunlight gleams on gun hilt

Cutting buckwheat—alone

Winter river—with a washboard I wash my clothes

"The sea used to be here" he says, as he tosses wood into the fire

It's so cold outside—I wish I had a hat

I eat mandarin oranges, warmed by a lovely fire

I wash my feet in complete darkness

Fisherman's house at noon—no chickens

Today the sea has calmed—we swim in the big river

Only people headed to work ride the trains today

Autumn leaves fall around the house—a face appears

There are no flowers on the graves these days

Moonlit night—the reeds break

Tomorrow is the first day of the year for both the Buddha and I

New Year's Eve—not even a bill collector visits

Snow piled up tonight—a lamp

From out of the rain, a boat approaches the shore

I watch the sun set, then pick up the chopsticks

Snowy winter forest, windows open everywhere

Opened window, laughing face

Shoreline—a small boat returns from nightfishing

Blind man on a windy road

A traveling couple makes plans

Working hard on a hot roof

A child who wants to draw pictures is here to play

I descend a windy mountain

Bare trees, spring rain, clouds come and go

Pine roots frozen and tinged with silver

The boat has emptied and everyone climbs aboard

Island snow—life on a small island

Solitary mountain—remnants of sunset

Return to the winter sky of my hometown

All day long it snows on both I and my neighbor

Fresh snowfall—footsteps appear

Full-page newspaper ad: "Spring is here!"

I wash the mud from my hands with rainwater

Dead, fallen branches—good for breaking

One quiet moment is drawn

On a meadow hill, blue wheat and a lone pine tree

Hard at work from dawn till dusk

Miserably poor, and yet a row of potted flowers

Melted frost, birds shimmer

The one-eyed tangerine salesman returns after a long time

Close the shōji—the wind speaks of dry reeds

Moonlit night—a stray cat is in love

Walking around town looking for work

Country tea house—hot rice on the stove

Snowfall at the end of spring

On the edge of a snowy forest

Thin meat from a thick bone

The tea strangles me—I set down the teacup

My thin body nestled at the window—boat's siren

Quite ill—willow's slender branches in the wind

Spring—smoke rises from behind a hill

Ten Translations of Georg Trakl

Trumpets

Under trimmed willows, brown children play
And leaves rustle, trumpets intone. Cemeteries tremble.
Scarlet banners reverberate through sycamore's grief,
Horsemen along rye fields, empty mills.

Or shepherds sing at night and stags step
Into the circle of fire, the groves' primitive sadness.
Dancers arise from a black wall,
Scarlet banners, laughter, insanity, trumpets.

DE PROFUNDIS

It is a stubble field where a black rain falls.
It is a brown tree that stands alone.
It is a hissing wind encircling empty houses—
How tragic is this evening.

Outside town
A gentle orphan gathers meager husks.
Her eyes, wide and golden, eat the dusk;
Her womb awaits the heavenly bridegroom.

Returning home,
Shepherds find the sweet corpse
Decaying in a thicket.

I am a shadow far from darkened villages.
I drink God's wordlessness
From a woodland well.

Cold metal forms on my forehead,
Spiders search for my heart.
In my mouth, a light is extinguished.

At night, I find myself in a field
Thick with filth and the dust of stars.
In a hazel thicket
Crystal angels sing again.

Amen

Depravity drifts through the disintegrating room,
Shadows on yellow draperies; in dark mirrors
The ivory sorrow of our hands refract.

Brown pearls drip through dead fingers.
Without words,
An angel's opium-blue eyes unclose.

And so the evening is blue.
The hour of our death; Azrael's shadow
Darkens a brown garden.

Decline
to Karl Borromäus Heinrich

Over the white pond
The wild birds have flown away.
At evening, an icy wind blows from our stars.

Over our graves
The broken bow of night descends.
Beneath oak trees we sway in a silver boat.

The white walls of the city ring forever.
Under arches of thorns,
O my brother, we blind hands of clocks climb towards midnight.

Summer

At evening, the song of the cuckoo
Grows silent in the forest.
The grain bows its head lower,
The red poppy.

Dark thunderclouds rise
Over the hill.
The cricket's ancient song
Dies in the field.

The leaves of the chestnut tree
Cease stirring.
Your dress rustles
On the spiral stair.

A candle gleams wordlessly
In the dark room;
A silver hand
Extinguishes the light;

Windless, starless night.

To the Child Elis

Elis, when the blackbirds call from the black wood,
This is your perdition.
Your lips drink the cool of the blue rockspring.

Let go, when your brow bleeds wordlessly,
Ancient legends
And dark interpretations of bird flight.

You walk with soft footsteps into night
Filled with purple grapes.
You move your arms more beautifully in the blue.

A thorn bush sings
Where are your lunar eyes.
O, how long, Elis, have you been dead.

Your body is a hyacinth
Into which a monk dips his waxen fingers.
Our silence is a black cavern

From which a gentle animal sometimes appears,
And slowly lowers its heavy eyelids.
Upon your temples black dew drips.

The final gold of fallen stars.

Elis

I.

Perfection is the stillness of this golden day.
Under ancient oaks
You, Elis, appear, reclining with round eyes.

Their blue reflects the slumber of lovers.
On your mouth
Their rosy sighs are stilled.

At evening, the fisherman hauls in his heavy nets.
A good shepherd
Leads his flock along the forest's edge.
O how righteous, Elis, are all your days.

The olive trees' blue stillness
Quietly descends on naked walls,
An old man's dark song dies away.

A golden boat sways,
Elis, your heart against a lonely sky.

II.

A gentle chime of bells rings in Elis' breast.
At evening
When his head sinks into a black pillow

A blue deer
Bleeds quietly in a thicket of thorns.

A brown tree stands there in solitude,
Its blue fruit fallen away.

Signs and stars
Sink, speechlessly vanish in the evening pond.

Behind the hill, winter has come.

At night
Blue doves drink the icy sweat
That flows from Elis' crystal brow.

On black walls
Forever drones the lonely wind of God.

Childhood

Full of fruit, an elderbush; childhood dwelt tranquil
In a blue cave. Over the bygone path
Where now the brown wildgrass sways,
Wordless branches ponder; the rustling leaves

Alike, as when blue water thunders under the crags.
The blackbird's lament is gentle. A shepherd
Speechlessly follows the sun that rolls down the autumnal hill.

A blue moment is pure soul.
At the forest's edge, a timid deer appears and peacefully
Old bells and somber hamlets rest in the valley.

Now devout, you know the purpose of dark years,
Coolness and autumn in empty rooms;
And shining footsteps sound out in holy blue.

Quietly an open window clatters; the sight
Of the neglected cemetery moves you to tears.
Recollections of ancient legends; yet the soul sometimes brightens
When it thinks of joyful people, the dark-gold days of spring.

Rest and Silence

Shepherds bury the sun in the skeletal forest.
With a net of hair
A fisherman hauls the moon from a frozen pond.

The pale moon dwells
In blue crystal, his face at rest among the stars.
Or he lowers his head in purple sleep

Yet the black flight of birds forever touches the watcher,
The fervor of blue flowers,
The local stillness ponders the forgotten, extinct angels.

Nightfall again envelops the brow among moonlit stones;
A radiant youth,
The sister appears in autumn and black decay.

Springtime of the Soul

Crying out in sleep, wind whips through the black alleys.
Blue spring beckons through the breaking boughs,
Purple night dew, and throughout the sky the stars extinguish.
Green river dawns, silver the old avenues
And the towers of the city. O gentle drunkenness
In the gliding boat, dark calls of the blackbird
In childlike gardens. The rose-red veil disperses.

The water murmurs solemnly. O the moist shadows on the meadow,
The striding animals; greenery, the blossoming branches
Touch the crystalline brow; shimmering rocking boat.
Wordlessly the sun sings in the rose-red mists on the hill.
Great is the stillness of the pine forest, the river's grave shadows.

Purity! Purity! Where are the terrible paths of the dying,
Of gray stony silence, the rocks of night
And the unquiet shadows? Radiant abyss of sunlight.

Sister, when I found you at noon
In the forest's lonely clearing, in the great silence of animals,
White under wild oak, the thorns flowered silver.
Massive death, and the singing flame in the heart.

Darker the waters flowed around the fish gracefully playing.
Hour of mourning, and the speechless gaze of the sun;
The soul is alien to earth. Ghostly twilight dims
Blue over the broken forest, and in the village
A bell tolls dark and long; they lead him to rest.
Silent the myrtle flowers of the white eyelids of the dead.

Quietly the water whispers in the afternoon's decline,
On the riverbank the green wilderness darkens,
                                      ecstasy in the rose-red wind,
The brother's quiet song by the evening hill.

Eric Hoffman is the author of several books of poetry, including *The Transparent Eye* (Spuyten Duyvil, 2016) and *Losses of Life* (Spuyten Duyvil, 2019). He lives in Connecticut with his wife Robin and son Sailor.